Washington was a Dancer, Lincoln was a Wrestler

Timothy D. Holder

Copyright © 2022 by
TDH Communications
Knoxville, TN

ISBN 979-8-9866410-0-3

Cover Design by Jill Holder

Art on cover by Currier & Ives, public domain

Note to Teachers and Parents:

Please feel free to make copies of the games.

For Jill,

who inspires me with her kindness, encouragement, insight, creativity, and love.

Acknowledgements

There are several people I appreciate for helping to turn the idea of this book into a reality.

I am grateful to Jill for the work she did on the cover. I think it looks outstanding. She also made great suggestions regarding content. This book benefitted from her insight and experience. She has such a strong background in children's literature and in working with kids that she really helped make this book better than it otherwise would have been.

I appreciate Tina Maddox for suggesting that I write a kids' book about presidents. It sounded outlandish to me at the time, but now it seems like the most natural fit in the world. She saw me doing this before I could see it myself. I have written more than a dozen books, but this is only the second one that came about because someone else suggested it. Having good friends who understand me— that is such a blessing.

I was inspired by people who heard about this book before it was written and said they wanted copies. That was encouraging.

Finally, it has been nice to have elementary school teachers invite me into their classrooms—and in one case, into their Zoom meeting—to share my love of presidents with their students. Each time, it was so much fun! And it helped inspire me to do this book.

Table of Contents

List of Presidents

Chapters

Games

List of Presidents

And When They Served

1 George Washington (1789-1797), 2 John Adams (1797-1801), 3 Thomas Jefferson (1801-1809),

4 James Madison (1809-1817), 5 James Monroe (1817-1825), 6 John Quincy Adams (1825-1829),

7 Andrew Jackson (1829-1837), 8 Martin Van Buren (1837-1841), 9 William Henry Harrison (1841),

10 John Tyler (1841-1845), 11 James Polk (1845-1849),

12 Zachary Taylor (1849-1850), 13 Millard Fillmore (1850-1853), 14 Franklin Pierce (1853-1857),

15 James Buchanan (1857-1861), 16 Abraham Lincoln (1861-1865), 17 Andrew Johnson (1865-1869),

18 Ulysses Grant (1869-1877), 19 Rutherford Hayes (1877-1881), 20 James Garfield (1881),

21 Chester Arthur (1881-1885), 22 Grover Cleveland (1885-1889), 23 Benjamin Harrison (1889-1893),

24 Grover Cleveland (1893-1897), 25 William McKinley (1897-1901), 26 Teddy Roosevelt (1901-1909),

27 William Howard Taft (1909-1913), 28 Woodrow Wilson (1913-1921), 29 Warren Harding (1921-1923),

30 Calvin Coolidge (1923-1929), 31 Herbert Hoover (1929-1933), 32 Franklin Roosevelt (1933-1945),

33 Harry Truman (1945-1953), 34 Dwight Eisenhower (1953-1961), 35 John Kennedy (1961-1963),

36 Lyndon Johnson (1963-1969), 37 Richard Nixon (1969-1974), 38 Gerald Ford (1974-1977),

39 Jimmy Carter (1977-1981), 40 Ronald Reagan (1981-1989), 41 George H. W. Bush (1989-1993),

42 Bill Clinton (1993-2001), 43 George W. Bush (2001-2009), 44 Barack Obama (2009-2017),

45 Donald Trump (2017-2021), 46 Joe Biden (2021-the present)

Washington was a Dancer, Lincoln was a Wrestler

Chapter One

Presidents and Their Pets

George Washington (1st president) loved horses. Thomas Jefferson (3rd president) said that Washington was better at riding horses than anybody. This was important to people back then. Everybody either rode horses, rode in wagons, or walked. People admired good horsemanship.

Jefferson complimented Washington even though Jefferson did not really like him. They used to be friends, but Jefferson did not like Washington's politics. When someone does not like another person, it can feel hard to compliment that person.

During the Revolution, Washington was going up a hill while riding a horse. The horse stepped in a small hole and started to fall. Washington pulled on the reins and kept the horse from falling. One of the soldiers said it was an amazing display of horsemanship. It also showed how strong Washington was. The soldier said he had never seen such an impressive thing.

Washington also had a bunch of hound dogs. He owned at least twelve. That sounds like a lot.

John Adams (2nd president) had a horse, too. Adams' horse had a unique name. Who calls their horse "Cleopatra"? John Adams did.

Adams also had two dogs. He called one "Juno". This is unusual but not strange. He called the other dog "Satan," which seems pretty strange to me.

Clearly, Adams was creative with pet names.

Some people say John Quincy Adams (6th president) had a pet alligator. He did not get it for himself. A French diplomat gave it to him. At least, that was the story. It was probably not true. Wouldn't it be something if it really happened?

The rumors started in the 1800s. But Adams kept a diary. He wrote in it a lot. He never wrote about a pet alligator.

If you had an alligator and a diary, don't you think you would write about it? I know I would.

Andrew Jackson (7th) had a parrot. He taught his parrot bad words. When Jackson's wife died, they had a funeral. During the funeral service, the bird started saying these bad words. It was embarrassing for everyone. This is one good reason not to teach a bird to say bad words. There are other reasons, too.

The King of Siam[1] wanted to give James Buchanan (15th) a herd of elephants. What would a president do with them?

Mail delivery was quite slow back then. By the time the king's letter made it to the White House, Abraham Lincoln (16th) was president. He did not know what to do with a herd of elephants. Someone said he could use them to help win the Civil War. Lincoln decided to just say "No, thank you" to the king.

Someone gave Lincoln's family a turkey to eat for Christmas. Lincoln did accept this gift. One of his sons liked the turkey, though, so they made it a pet instead of dinner.

James Garfield (20th) had a dog named "Veto." He also had a sense of humor. ("He," meaning the president, not the dog.) A veto is what a president does when he is

---

[1] Thailand used to be called Siam.

against a bill that Congress is trying to pass. A veto stops a bill from becoming a law. Doing this can be controversial, so Garfield was making a joke that he was not afraid of a veto.

Sometimes presidents make jokes that are not funny. Garfield seemed pretty funny though.

Theodore Roosevelt (26th) had a pet bear that he named "Jonathan Edwards." This was the name of a famous preacher from the 1700s. Which seems stranger to you—having a pet bear or naming it after a preacher?

Woodrow Wilson (28th) had some sheep.

Calvin Coolidge (30th) owned a raccoon named "Rebecca." He would take her on walks. She was safe though because she was on a leash.

Checkers was a famous presidential pet. Years before Richard Nixon (37th) became president, he was the vice president for Dwight Eisenhower (34th). When Nixon was running for VP, someone gave him a dog. The politician gave it to his daughters. One of them named the dog "Checkers".

Later, Democrats accused Nixon of taking bribes. He got on TV and defended his honor. He said the only gift he ever failed to mention was Checkers. He said he would keep Checkers. His speech became known as the "Checkers Speech." Sometimes history books talk about it.

Ronald Reagan (40th) never had a pet chimpanzee. However, he did star in a movie with a chimp named "Bonzo." Reagan played a professor. In the movie, the professor hired a nanny to help him raise the chimp. The movie, *Bedtime for Bonzo*, was a comedy.

There was a sequel, but it had a different star and a different chimp.

Bill Clinton (42nd) had a cat named "Socks". Socks was a stray the Clintons adopted. Wasn't that nice of them?

Barack Obama (44th) had a dog he called "Bo". "BO" are also Obama's initials. I wonder if that is a coincidence.

Chapter Two

Presidential Athletes

George Washington was an excellent dancer. One time, he danced for three hours. Does dancing for hours seem athletic to you? Have you ever tried it? I have never danced that long. I bet it would be exhausting. Washington was strong and graceful. Women loved dancing with him.

Washington was also good at throwing things. In the 1700s, men showed how strong they were by seeing who could throw the farthest. They threw rocks, metal bars, and other stuff. Typically, Washington won these competitions. Once during the Revolutionary War, a group of young soldiers were throwing a bar. Washington made the longest throw on his first try without stretching or warming up. The soldiers encouraged him to do it again. He said if one of them could beat his first throw, then he would. And he walked away.

George Washington was remarkable.

They say Abraham Lincoln was an amazing wrestler. He is actually in the National Wrestling Hall of Fame. He won 299 wrestling matches. He only lost one that we know of. Can you imagine having a won-lost record of 299-1 in anything? That is amazing.

But Lincoln did not look for trouble. He once locked himself in a room to avoid a man who wanted to fight. The man threatened to break through the door to get to him. Lincoln climbed out a window to get away.

Abraham Lincoln was an interesting fellow.

Grover Cleveland (22nd and 24th president) was not overly athletic. When he was president, a boy was born whose parents named him after Cleveland. The boy was Grover Cleveland Alexander. He was a great athlete. Alexander was a pitcher in Major League Baseball. He played for the Phillies, Cubs, and Cardinals. He won 373 games! That is tied for the third best all-time for pitchers. This is a great example of irony: an amazing athlete being named after someone who was not athletic.

For some reason, Alexander's nickname was "Old Pete."

Theodore Roosevelt liked being physically fit. One way he exercised was by taking fast walks. Instead of having all his meetings while sitting around a table, some of them would take place as he walked swiftly through the streets of Washington DC. There were men who had to meet with him who were older and out of shape. They did not enjoy the walking meetings.

Roosevelt also liked boxing. Sometimes he would spar with amateurs. Other times he would box with professionals. That seems scary, but Roosevelt was a brave man.

Boxing can be dangerous. One day Roosevelt was boxing with an Army officer. The officer was supposed to keep the president safe. But the officer accidentally hit Roosevelt too hard on the side of the head. The president went blind in one eye. Roosevelt never told the man that he was the one who blinded him. The president did not want him to feel bad.

Wasn't that kind of Roosevelt? If a guy blinded me in one eye, I might have a hard time thinking about his feelings in that moment.

Roosevelt also practiced martial arts when he was president. One day at an outdoor lunch, he threw a diplomat to the ground to show the man the latest move Roosevelt had learned.

Dwight Eisenhower enjoyed many sports. Eisenhower played football in college. He went to West Point. Years later, he played a lot of golf. He loved it so much that he and his wife bought a house that was within walking distance of a golf course. One time he invited Nixon to play with him.

Is it funny to think of a president and a future president playing golf together?

John Kennedy (35th) became president right after Eisenhower. Kennedy played football for Harvard. He never made it onto the varsity team though. He had several health issues. That made it hard for him to play his best.

Richard Nixon was another president who was a big fan of football. In high school, he was an offensive lineman. When he was president, he drew up a play and gave it to the coach of the Washington Redskins.[2] Washington ran the president's play during a playoff game. They lost yardage and never tried it again.

They also never asked Nixon for any more ideas.

Gerald Ford (38th) was extremely good at football. He was the center on his college team, the University of Michigan. Two NFL teams were interested in him. The Green Bay Packers and the Detroit Lions wanted him. Nowadays, the National Football League drafts college players. Back then they did not. These two teams just offered him a contract.

Football was not as popular back then as it is today, so the players did not make very much money. Ford did not think playing football was a good option for him after college. The sport still ended up helping him though. He

---

[2] The Washington Commanders used to be called the Redskins.

became an assistant coach for the football team at Yale University. That paid for him to study law there. He became a lawyer and then a politician.

Ford also loved to play golf. He once hit a hole in one! Wouldn't that be cool?

Ford was very serious about golf. One time a reporter wanted to interview Ford about another president. The other president was involved in a scandal. Ford had little to say about that. Mostly, Ford wanted to talk about how the other president cheated at golf.

Ronald Reagan played football in a movie. He also played it in real life. Like Nixon and Ford, he played on the offensive line. Do you think it is funny that all three men were offensive linemen? It might not be funny, but it is interesting.

Reagan played at Eureka College. This school is in Illinois.

George H. W. Bush (41st) played baseball in college. He was not as successful at baseball as Ford was at football, but they were both quite good at their sports. Bush played for Yale University. He was a first baseman.

He got to play in the first two College World Series. I bet that was fun.

As president, he liked to play golf, which is something several other presidents enjoyed.

Bill Clinton liked to jog when he was president. This presented a challenge for the Secret Service. The Secret Service is assigned to protect the president. Because Clinton wanted to jog, the Secret Service had to have agents who could jog, too. They had to keep up with the president. They had to do that while carrying a gun and a radio. They also had to keep looking around to make sure the president was safe.

Clinton was quite friendly. This made the job of the Secret Service even harder. He liked to talk to strangers. When other joggers would see the president, they wanted to jog along with him. He loved that. But the Secret Service did not love it. They could never be sure if another jogger secretly wanted to hurt him.

George W. Bush (43rd) was not as good at baseball as his dad was. But the second President Bush used to be the part owner of a Major League Baseball team, the Texas Rangers, for a while.

Barack Obama is such a fan of college basketball that he filled out a bracket each March. Do you know what a college basketball bracket is? At the end of every college basketball season, a bunch of teams are invited to a tournament to see which team is the best. They are all placed in a bracket that simply shows which teams are playing against each other in the first round. Then it shows who the winners play in the next round and the next. It outlines all the games until a champion is crowned.

Some basketball fans fill out brackets where they guess which teams will win and advance to the next rounds.

Obama filled out a bracket even when he was super busy as president.

Chapter Three

George Trivia

All the trivia on this page is about the three presidents named George. They are George Washington, George H. W. Bush, and George W. Bush.

Do you know which George was born in Virginia? It was the first one—George Washington. You can visit his home in Mount Vernon. They offer tours there.

George Washington's wife was Martha. She had the same first name as Superman's mom and Batman's mom. I think that is kind of cool.

Washington was the only president among the Georges who had stepchildren. Their names were Jacky and Patsy. They loved him, and he loved them.

George Herbert Walker Bush was the husband of Barbara. They were married for 73 years! They met at a Christmas dance when they were in high school.

Several years before he was president, George H. W. Bush was the Director of the CIA.

George H. W. Bush is the only one of these men to serve just one term. For a while he was really popular as president. When the economy went bad, people became unhappy with him.

George W. Bush's wife is named Laura. She was a teacher and then a librarian. Can you imagine if your school librarian became the wife of a president?

George W. Bush is the only president with that first name who did not fight in a war. He was in the Texas Air National Guard during the Vietnam War, but he stayed in the USA for his military service. He never actually fought in Vietnam.

Chapter Four

James Trivia

There are six presidents named James. They are James Madison (4th), James Monroe (5th), James Polk (11th), James Buchanan, James Garfield, and James Carter (39th). James Carter was usually called "Jimmy".

Among this group of presidents, James Madison was the closest friend to George Washington. They worked together as politicians. Sometimes Madison wrote important papers for Washington. This was not like if someone wrote your paper for a class. A lot of politicians have speechwriters. Politicians also have people write papers explaining where the politician stands on an issue. Madison was so smart that a lot of politicians wanted his help.

James Madison and James Monroe were friends, but sometimes they were rivals. Madison and Monroe once ran against each other for a seat in the House of Representatives. Madison won.

Sometimes people get Madison and Monroe confused. They served back-to-back as presidents. Madison was the fourth one. Monroe was the fifth. They have the same first names obviously. Their last names both begin with "M." They are both from Virginia. They both were friends with Thomas Jefferson.

People did not get them confused back then though. Madison was one of the smartest men in the country. Monroe was smart too, but he was not as smart as Madison. Madison was a good friend to some people, but he tended to be shy. Monroe was outgoing. Madison was kind of sickly and was not a soldier. Monroe was tall and strong and fought in the Revolutionary War.

James Polk was born in North Carolina, but he moved to Tennessee.

He was president during the war between Mexico and the USA.

Most presidents want to be in office for two full terms. That would add up to eight years. James Polk said he would only serve one term. He promised this because he did not expect to be president at all. Democrats argued over two candidates and could not agree on which one to pick. Neither side wanted to give in. Neither side wanted the other candidate. As a compromise, both sides settled for Polk. He was shocked. He had hoped he might get picked as the vice presidential candidate.

After his four years in office, he did not run again.

James Buchanan was the only president so far who never married. He was engaged once. The woman broke off the engagement. She died a little while after that. Her dad was really mad at Buchanan. He would not let Buchanan come to the funeral. We do not know what the man was so mad about.

President Garfield was the only president named James who got shot while he was president.[3] Doctors back then did not know as much about medicine as they do today. They were not able to save him. When his assassin was put on trial, he said he was not guilty of murder. He only shot the President. The assassin said the doctors were responsible for killing Garfield.

The jury disagreed. The man was found guilty.

---

[3] Monroe was shot during the Revolutionary War.

James "Jimmy" Carter is the only president with this first name who served in the United States Navy. For a while, he was assigned to a submarine. Would you want to serve on a submarine?

Carter was also the only president who made his living for a while as a peanut farmer. Did you know that people grow peanuts on farms?

Chapter Five

John Trivia

There are four presidents named John. They are John Adams, John Quincy Adams, John Tyler (9ᵗʰ), and John Kennedy.

John Adams was the only one of these four to never serve in Congress. When the United States Government was first created, Adams was elected vice president. Later, he was elected president. After that, he retired.

John Quincy Adams had several interesting jobs in the government besides being president. He started as a diplomat. Later, he was a senator and then secretary of state. After he was done being president, he got elected to the House of Representatives. Usually, politicians move from their positions when they can take a job with more authority. Adams moved to a position of less authority. He did not pursue the House position. Leaders in his community asked him to run for that office. I bet that made him feel good. Instead of looking at it as a demotion, he could see it as his neighbors having respect for him.

Two of these presidents switched political parties. John Quincy Adams was a Federalist. The Federalists formed the first political party. They existed before there was a Republican or Democratic Party. Eventually, the Federalist Party fell apart. This happened because most Americans did not agree with their views. The Federalists controlled the government, and they tried to take away the right of free speech. When they did this, many Americans turned against them.

John Quincy Adams thought the Federalists were mean to his father, John Adams. There were other things that bothered John Q. Adams about the Federalist Party, too, so he became a Democratic-Republican.

Strangely, there used to be a Democratic-Republican Party, and today there is a Democratic Party and a Republican Party. Life is funny sometimes. The Democratic-Republican Party became the Democratic Party. I think that was a good idea. "Democratic-Republican" is a long title. That is a lot of syllables.

John Tyler used to be a Democrat, but he did not like how Andrew Jackson acted. Tyler became a Whig because he was against Jackson, who was the leader of the Democratic Party back then.

The Whig Party in America got its name from the Whig Party in Britain. Over there, the Whigs wanted to limit the power of the king. Some Americans thought Andrew Jackson was acting like a king. These people took the name "Whigs" to show what they thought of Jackson.

It is interesting that some people switched parties because they did not like how other people behaved. Nowadays, people usually switch parties because of the policies of the parties.

Three of these presidents were born in Massachusetts. The only one who was born elsewhere was John Tyler. He was from Virginia.

Surprisingly, Tyler sided with the South right before the Civil War. Here is why this was surprising: The Civil War happened because some southern states left the US government and formed their own country. Their reasons for leaving, and the reasons why the United States (the Union) wanted them back are complicated. But you would expect someone who was President of the United States to always be loyal to the USA. Tyler was more loyal to Virginia than he was to the United States.

All four of these men were comfortable financially, but John Kennedy was by far the richest of them. His father made money from a lot of different things.

Chapter Six

William Trivia

There are four presidents who were named William. We had William "Bill" Clinton, William Henry Harrison (9th), William McKinley (25th), and William Howard Taft (27th). There was also a William who ran for president three times but never won. His name was William Jennings Bryan.

Of all these Williams, only Clinton and McKinley were elected president twice.

Another interesting fact about McKinley is he was president during the Spanish-American War. This war was fought in Cuba. Cuba used to be controlled by Spain, but the Cubans wanted to be free. The United States supported Cuba. The war started and ended for the US in 1898. The Cubans had been fighting the Spanish long before that. The US and Cuba won.

William Henry Harrison was the only man mentioned on this page who knew Thomas Jefferson personally. Harrison was an army officer, so Jefferson was his boss. The president is the commander-in-chief of the military.

The Cowardly Lion character from *The Wizard of Oz* was inspired by William Jennings Bryan. The lion had a powerful roar, and Bryan was a great public speaker. The author of the book wanted Bryan to speak up and challenge McKinley more. Bryan was the better speaker, but McKinley won elections against him twice.

William Howard Taft had a tough time as president. One time, he got stuck in a White House bathtub. It happened because he was very overweight. A lot of people thought it was funny. Laughing at people because they are overweight is not very nice though.

When he ran for reelection, he finished in third place. Some presidents have finished their term and decided not to run again. When presidents do run for a second term, they have always finished first or second, except for Taft. He was conservative, so liberals did not like him. He did not fight for conservative issues because he thought Congress should make decisions without his input. This made many conservatives think he did not really care about their issues. Taft did care, but he thought the role of the president in the government should be limited.

William Henry Harrison was a Whig. The Whigs did not like Andrew Jackson, remember? That said, Harrison was kind of like Jackson. Both were considered war heroes. Neither had much political experience before becoming president.

There was a president named William who was from Arkansas. It was Clinton. He was born in the town of Hope. When he ran for president, he had a video called "A Man from Hope".

William Jennings Bryan and Bill Clinton were Democrats. William McKinley and William Howard Taft were Republicans.

Harrison and McKinley died in office. Harrison got sick, but McKinley was assassinated. Taft and Clinton did not die in office.

Chapter Seven

Musical Presidents

Thomas Jefferson loved to make music with his sister. They performed hymns and other songs. Jefferson enjoyed the work of classical composers. He liked Handel and Vivaldi in particular. One of the instruments he played was the cello. He also enjoyed playing the violin. But the third president was not just an instrumentalist. He really enjoyed singing too.

John Quincy Adams was a flutist. He also used to write songs. Does it surprise you that a president was a song writer? It surprised me.

John Tyler played the violin. He stopped so he could devote more time to studying to be a lawyer. I can relate to that. I played the harmonica, but I decided to give it up to focus on being a writer. After Tyler retired, he started playing the violin again.
Who knows? Maybe I will go back to playing the harmonica someday.

Just like Thomas Jefferson and John Tyler, Abraham Lincoln used to play the violin.

William McKinley loved to sing hymns. His faith was important to him.

Calvin Coolidge could play the harmonica. I think that is pretty neat! I wonder if his pet raccoon enjoyed it.

Harry Truman (33rd) and Richard Nixon were both exceptional piano players. Nixon was good at several other instruments too. The most interesting one might be the accordion. Nixon was yet another president who could play the violin.

Even though Nixon played many instruments, he could not read music. He played everything by ear.

Bill Clinton loved the saxophone. He played it when he was a student in school. When he was running for president, he played it on a late night talk show. He did this as a guest on *The Arsenio Hall Show*.

Barack Obama was not afraid to sing in public. In 2012, he performed part of the song "Let's Stay Together". On a different occasion, he sang part of "Sweet Home Chicago". You can watch a clip of this on YouTube.

Chapter Eight

Presidential Faith

Both George Washington and Ronald Reagan got shot at. Washington was not hit but Reagan was. The two men survived. They both believed God saved them for a special purpose.

General Washington was a vestryman in his church. A vestryman was like a deacon but also kind of different. A vestryman had more responsibilities than a deacon. The vestrymen made sure the preacher was paid. They also took care of the needy in the community, among other responsibilities.

When James Madison was a young man, he thought about becoming a preacher. Instead, he became a lawyer. Later he became a politician, of course. Though he did not become a preacher, he did learn how to read Hebrew. He wanted to read the Old Testament in the original language. He was curious about how a group of people created a government for themselves. This is what the Israelites did, as recorded in the Old Testament. Madison thought reading their story in the original language would give him a deeper understanding of the creation of their government.

James K. Polk was committed to the Methodist Church. His wife was a serious Presbyterian. Every Sunday, when they worshipped together, they always went to the Presbyterian Church. If Mrs. Polk was sick or out of town, Polk would go to a Methodist Church.

Abraham Lincoln never officially joined a church. But during the Civil War, he quoted the Bible a lot. And he attended a Presbyterian Church.

James Garfield was a minister. He belonged to the Disciples of Christ Church. He accomplished a lot. In addition to being a preacher, he spent time as a professor. He was also a college president and a Civil War general. All of that was before he became president.

William McKinley was committed to Christianity. His mother hoped he would become a Methodist bishop someday. In the Methodist Church, the bishop is the boss of a group of preachers in a given area.

Theodore Roosevelt belonged to the Dutch Reformed Church. While in college, he taught a Sunday School class. His class was in an Episcopal Church. When Roosevelt was a senior, the church got a new leader. He wanted Roosevelt to officially join his church. It makes sense that an Episcopal leader would want Episcopalians to teach Episcopalians in his church. But Roosevelt refused. He chose to stay a part of the Dutch Reformed Church. The leader fired him. Roosevelt just started a class in a different church.

Woodrow Wilson was serious enough about his Presbyterian faith that he was a ruling elder in his church.

Herbert Hoover (31st) and Richard Nixon were the only two presidents who were Quakers. Quakers are usually pacifists. A pacifist is someone who refuses to fight. Despite this, Nixon served in World War Two. Nixon could have avoided military service because of his faith. He served anyway.

Dwight Eisenhower got baptized into the Presbyterian Church. He did this only ten days after he was inaugurated as president. He came from a family of Mennonites. People of this faith are usually pacifists. Eisenhower's lengthy military service made his continued allegiance to that church awkward. He was a Jehovah's Witness for many years before eventually becoming a Presbyterian.

John Kennedy and Joe Biden (46th) are the only two Catholic presidents in American history. A lot of Americans used to not like Catholics. Some people feared that a Catholic president would take orders from the Pope. Obviously, most Americans stopped feeling this way. The proof? Kennedy and Biden got elected.

Jimmy Carter was very committed to the Baptist Church. He taught Sunday School for many years. He did this a lot longer than Theodore Roosevelt did. Carter tried to set a moral example. He promised voters he would not tell lies as president. He ran for president in 1976. This was right after presidents had lied about Vietnam and Watergate. After he finished being president, Carter still tried to do something good. He helped build houses for a charity called Habitat for Humanity.

Chapter Nine

Presidential Fighters

George Washington fought in two wars before he became president. He was in the French and Indian War. He was part of the Virginia militia. He wanted to be an officer in the British Army. The British let him serve with them as an advisor. But they did not make him a British officer. He was still just a Virginia Militiaman. The French and Indian War lasted from 1754-1763. The British and Americans won the war against the French and the Native American allies of the French.

In 1775, Washington became the commander-in-chief of the Continental Army in the Revolutionary War. He was not the only future president in this war. James Monroe also served in Washington's army.

Alexander Hamilton fought in the Revolution too. He was never a president, but he was famous. He was also Washington's close friend. Maybe you saw the musical about Hamilton.

James Monroe was wounded during the Battle of Trenton during the Revolution. He was shot by a Hessian soldier. The Hessians fought on the side of the British. Monroe was wounded after he crossed the Delaware with Washington and the Continental Army.

Andrew Jackson fought in the War of 1812 against the British. This war lasted from 1812-1815. Jackson was most famous for winning the Battle of New Orleans. There is even a song about it.

Jackson was also known for fighting against the Native Americans.

William Henry Harrison was another future president who was in the War of 1812. He is mostly remembered for fighting Native Americans, but he fought battles against the British too.

I am glad we do not fight the British anymore.

Zachary Taylor (12th) was a hero in the Mexican War. This war was from 1845-1848. His troops nicknamed him "Old Rough and Ready". They called him this because he was willing to go through the mud and dirt with them. He did not try to keep himself clean and removed from his men.

Franklin Pierce (14th) was another veteran of the Mexican War. During his presidential campaign, some of his political enemies argued that he was not worthy to be president. They said he was a coward because he missed a big battle during that war. His political party, the Democrats, supported him. But what is interesting is that some of his political enemies supported him, too. They said they did not like his politics, but he was a brave man and deserved the country's respect.

Can you imagine if Republicans said nice things about Biden? Can you imagine if Democrats said something kind about Trump (45th)? It is amazing that some of Pierce's political enemies defended his honor.

Abraham Lincoln was in the Illinois Militia during the Blackhawk War in 1832. This was between the United States military and some Native Americans. The whole war was over in less than five months. It went from April to August in 1832. Lincoln was the captain of his military company, but he was not in any actual battles.

Ulysses Grant (18th) was, like Washington, in two wars. Grant served in the Mexican War. He gained valuable experience in warfare there. Later, Grant led the Union Army in the Civil War. This war lasted from 1861-1865. Grant learned that a key to winning in war was to not quit. If you just keep going, you can usually win. This can be applied to a lot of things.

Five future presidents fought in the Civil War. In addition to Grant, there was Rutherford B. Hayes (19th), James Garfield, Benjamin Harrison (23rd), and William McKinley. They were all Republicans. They all fought on the Union side.

Theodore Roosevelt was in the Spanish-American War. It was not easy for him to get into the fighting. It was over quickly. It started and ended in 1898. Roosevelt was the assistant secretary of the Navy when it started. He resigned from his government job and joined the Army. He was assigned to the fighting in Cuba and faced the enemy in combat. He was a war hero.

Harry Truman served in World War One. This war started in Europe and lasted from 1914 to 1918. The USA was only in it from 1917-1918. Truman was a captain in the Army. He fought on the front lines in Europe. He was the only future president to fight in this war. Dwight Eisenhower was also in the Army during World War One, but he was stationed somewhere else.

Many future presidents fought in World War Two. The USA was in the war from 1941-1945. The fighting started in Europe in September 1939. Japan and China were fighting right before that.

Dwight Eisenhower oversaw the Allied military in North Africa. Later, Eisenhower led the military in Europe. Eisenhower fought against the Germans and Italians.

John Kennedy served in Europe before fighting in the Pacific. Kennedy was in the Navy. He was on a boat that the Japanese destroyed. He swam to a nearby island with the other sailors in his crew. They were rescued by their fellow Americans a few days later.

Lyndon Johnson served in the Naval Reserves in World War Two. He spent part of his time in Washington DC. He helped organize the shipment of supplies to the military. He also spent time in the Pacific, and he flew on some bomber planes.

Richard Nixon served in the Navy. He was assigned to fight in the Pacific. Nixon was humble about his service. He said he was far away from the front lines. He mostly grilled hamburgers and learned how to play card games, he said.

Gerald Ford served on a ship in the Pacific. He had been a lawyer before the war. After the Japanese attack on Pearl Harbor, he decided to enlist. A lot of men gave up jobs to serve their country. That was noble of them.

Jimmy Carter was in college at the Naval Academy. He was not in the Navy yet. He was only training to be, so he was a cadet. He spent a couple of summers at sea during the war. One time, he was in the Pacific. A big wave came over the side of the ship. It hit Cadet Carter and knocked him thirty feet across the deck! If the ship had been turned sideways from the wave, he would have gone overboard. Because the storm and the waves were so loud, his cries for help would probably not have been heard. He would have been lost at sea.

Carter graduated from the Naval Academy in 1946, but the war ended in 1945.

The last future president to serve in World War Two was George H. W. Bush. He was a fighter pilot. Bush was once shot down by the Japanese. Fortunately, Americans rescued him before he got captured or drowned in the ocean.

The Korean war was from 1950-1953. Harry Truman was president when it started. Dwight Eisenhower was president by the time it ended. No future presidents fought in this one.

George W. Bush was a military pilot like his father. The younger George Bush served during the Vietnam War. But he did not fight in that conflict. He did all his flying in the USA. Not everybody who serves in the military during a war goes overseas to fight.

Chapter Ten

Presidential Friendships

George Washington was good friends with John Adams. Their friendship was strong even though they were very different. Washington read a lot, but he did not have much formal education. John Adams was quite well-educated. He went to Harvard. Washington was reserved, but Adams was passionate. Adams was a great speaker. Washington was uncomfortable talking in front of large groups. A lot of people feel the same as Washington. Many people don't like public speaking. I think it is a great thing to do.

Anyway, Washington liked Adams and found him interesting. But Adams was not Washington's only friend who became a president. Washington was also close with James Madison. Washington admired Madison. The feeling was mutual. Madison was impressed by Washington's leadership and character. Washington recognized that Madison was brilliant and trustworthy. They worked well together.

John Adams and Thomas Jefferson were good friends. They respected each other. Both men were patriots. They were extremely smart. Jefferson admired Adams for being so good at giving speeches. Adams thought Jefferson was an excellent writer.

Then they got mad at each other. A journalist made up mean things about Adams. Adams and his wife Abigail asked Jefferson to tell the man to stop. Adams and his wife thought the man would listen to Jefferson. They believed this because the journalist and Jefferson belonged to the same political party. Jefferson was a Democratic-

41

Republican. Adams was a Federalist. Jefferson refused to confront the man, and that hurt his friends' feelings. Both John and Abigail were upset.

Jefferson was the vice president when Adams was president. One time, Adams asked Jefferson to go to France and talk through a problem. Jefferson agreed at first, but then he changed his mind. He decided that he did not want to help Adams' political party. Understandably, Adams was unhappy about this.

Years later, Abigail Adams died. Jefferson wrote a sympathetic letter to her husband John. John Adams replied with his own lengthy and kind letter. After this, the two men became friends again. They wrote each other many more letters after that.

Jefferson was good friends with James Madison. Madison had a great ability at teaming up with influential people and doing big things. Both Jefferson and Madison were brilliant. They also shared the political belief that the national government should not be too powerful. They started a political party together. As mentioned before, it was the Democratic-Republican Party. Today, it is known as the Democratic Party.

Jefferson and James Monroe were excellent friends. Monroe bought land next to Jefferson's plantation so they could be neighbors.

Andrew Jackson really liked James Polk. Both men were from Tennessee. Jackson's nickname was "Old Hickory" because he was tough, like a piece of hickory wood. People called Polk "Young Hickory" because he was such a close follower of Jackson.

Theodore Roosevelt was quite close with William Howard Taft. When Roosevelt decided he would not run for reelection in 1908, he said people should vote for Taft instead. Taft was elected president. But then Roosevelt did not like how Taft was doing his job. Roosevelt got mad and decided to run in the election of 1912 against him. This hurt Taft's feelings.

Neither man won the 1912 election. Woodrow Wilson beat them.

A few years later, the two men made up and became friends again. When Roosevelt died, Taft talked at the funeral about how glad he was that they had fixed their friendship.

John Kennedy and Richard Nixon were friends, or at least they were friendly at times. This was nice since they were from different political parties. They were also from different parts of the country and had different backgrounds. Kennedy was born into a rich family in Massachusetts. Nixon's family did not have much money and lived in California. Nixon was shy and awkward. He admired how easily Kennedy got along with people. Kennedy was impressed by how smart Nixon was. They respected each other, and they thought they could learn from each other. It hurt their friendship when they were opponents in the presidential election of 1960. Kennedy won that year. Nixon thought that there was some cheating that happened. Unfortunately for Nixon, he could not prove this.

George H. W. Bush and Bill Clinton only became friends after they were rivals. Bush ran against Clinton for the presidency in 1992. The two men did not like each other then. They became friends after they were both done being president. They worked together to help people after a natural disaster struck in Asia. This was when their friendship was born.

Barack Obama and Joe Biden seem to get along well. People have created memes about their bond. Presidents and vice presidents are not always friends, so it is nice that these two like each other.

Chapter Eleven

Outer Space Presidents

No president has ever been in outer space. It has not happened before, during, or after they were president. But wouldn't it be cool if one of them had been an astronaut?

Dwight Eisenhower started our space program. That happened back in the 1950s.

In the 1960s, John Kennedy said we should go to the moon. He believed we could get there by the end of the decade. He thought it would help our space program to have a specific goal. And we did it! We put men on the moon by 1969.
It helps to have goals.

Richard Nixon was the president during all our moon landings. We had six of them. The first one was in July 1969. Twenty-four men went to the moon altogether. Only twelve were able to get out of their spaceships and walk on it. It would be tough to go all the way to the moon and not get out of the spaceship. The last moon landing (so far) was in December 1972.

John Glenn was an astronaut who ran for president. On February 20, 1962, Glenn flew into space. He was the third person to orbit the earth. He was the first American. The two men before him were from Russia.
Glenn wanted to be the candidate for the Democratic Party in 1984. If he had won the Democratic nomination, he would have run against Ronald Reagan. Glenn was not chosen by his party. It was probably for the

best. Reagan had already been president for four years, and most voters liked him. When he ran for reelection in 1984, Reagan won forty-nine out of fifty states.

When Donald Trump was president, he started the Space Force. It is now a branch of the military. The other branches are the Army, Navy, Air Force, Marines, and Coast Guard. The newest branch of the military focuses on technology and threats in and from space. This does not mean that Trump was worried about aliens. He was concerned with other countries improving their technology. Trump did not want those countries to be able to do things in outer space that the USA could not do.

Chapter Twelve

Left-Handed Presidents

Around ten percent of all Americans are lefthanded. There have been at least six lefty presidents. Maybe there were more. Here are the lefthanded presidents we know about:

James Garfield
Herbert Hoover
Gerald Ford
George H. W. Bush
Bill Clinton
Barack Obama

Harry Truman and Ronald Reagan were ambidextrous. That means they could use both their right and left hands well.

There might have been other lefthanded presidents. In the old days, some people did not like it when kids were lefthanded. Many lefthanded people were forced to favor their right hands. Thus, some presidents might have been lefties, but no one knew it.

When my grandfather was in third grade, his teacher spanked him for writing with his left hand. Isn't that sad?

Outside of America there are still many people who don't like left handedness. I am glad we do not think that way in the USA anymore.

Chapter Thirteen

Presidential Myths

One myth about presidents involves a man who was not one: Benjamin Franklin. Some people think he was a president because he is so famous. He probably would have gotten elected if he was younger.

After the American Revolution, the two most popular men in the country were Washington and Franklin. Washington became the first president in 1789. Franklin was 83 years old that year. He died in 1790. If Franklin had been younger, he probably would have been elected after Washington finished serving his two terms.

There is a famous story about George Washington chopping down a cherry tree. The story goes something like this: When Washington was a little boy, he chopped down a cherry tree on his property. His dad discovered what had happened and asked who did it. Young George said he could not tell a lie. He admitted that he chopped down the tree.

In the original story, the youngster just damaged the tree with his new hatchet. He was 6 years old, so chopping a tree down would have been quite a feat. But as the story has been retold through the ages, people usually say the tree was cut down.

Anyway, his father was touched by the boy's honesty and said such virtue was worth more than a thousand trees.

Only three parts of this story are true. One, there are trees in Virginia. Two, there was a boy named George Washington. Three, his dad appreciated it when George told the truth.

Other than that, this tale is a work of fiction. There was an author, Mason Weems, who wanted to use the life of Washington to communicate moral lessons to the young people of America. Weems made up stories but called his work a biography.

The point of the cherry tree tale is that honesty is a virtue, but the story itself is a lie. This is a wonderful example of irony.

Another myth involving Washington is that he had wooden teeth. This is not exactly true. Washington had false teeth, but they were not made of wood. Wood is not a good choice for false teeth. Wood gets soft and mushy when it is wet. Wooden teeth would get soggy pretty quickly.

Washington had tried to take care of his regular teeth, but he had a lot of problems. He had to have teeth pulled while he was still in his twenties. Over the years, he had several sets of dentures. They were made of different substances, including ivory, silver, and copper. There were also animal teeth mixed in. Walrus, cow, and horse teeth were used. There were even human teeth. On one set of Washington's dentures, there were two human incisors.

Where did the human teeth come from?

We do not know. Dentists back then would pay people for their teeth. Poor people and slaves could sell a few of their teeth when they needed money. The dentist's patients would not know where the teeth came from. It's kind of like today when a surgery patient needs a blood transfusion during an operation. The patient usually does not know who the blood is provided by. The blood is donated by someone who gets paid for it. The difference, obviously, is that our bodies can create more blood after we make a donation. If a permanent tooth is pulled, a new tooth does not grow in its place.

Can you imagine having animal teeth in your mouth? Can you imagine having another person's teeth? George Washington had a much different life than we do.

When Thomas Jefferson was in a presidential race, some political enemies said he was an atheist. This was false. It is true that Jefferson was not very religious. He was an Episcopalian, but he was not very involved in his church. He also did not believe the traditional teachings of Christianity about Jesus.

Jefferson was a Deist. Deists believed that some kind of God must have created the universe, but they did not believe miracles occurred after that. Christianity teaches that Jesus performed miracles and rose from the dead. Jefferson did not accept that. Jefferson believed that Christianity was useful because it taught good morals. He believed that Jesus was a good teacher and a nice role model. Jefferson said he was a Christian, but he believed other Christians had made up all the stuff about miracles.

An atheist believes that there is no Creator God. Atheists do not believe in the supernatural. Because they do not believe in God or the supernatural, atheists also do not believe in miracles. Jefferson had that one belief in common with atheists—he did not believe in miracles. But he believed in God, so he was not an atheist. His views contradicted traditional Christianity, but he was not an atheist.

I already wrote about the story of John Quincy Adams and his alligator in the chapter on presidential pets. We do not need to go over it again, but it might be my favorite presidential myth.

Adams had a personality that could be pretty difficult. I imagine that people who did not like him got a big laugh about the idea of Adams with an alligator. They probably figured a mean guy like Adams would not be

50

content with a cuddly cat or a loyal and loving dog. I bet they thought a mean and scary guy deserved a mean and scary pet.

Please note, I am not saying Adams was a bad person. I am saying his enemies said he was not very nice.

There is a myth about Abraham Lincoln that you might not have heard. I have been studying presidents for many years, and I had never heard it. Some people tried to discredit Lincoln by saying he owned slaves at one time. This is nonsense.

Lincoln grew up in poverty. His family was much too poor to own slaves. Lincoln became a lawyer who spoke out against slavery. There was no evidence that he owned slaves. And there was no practical reason for him to feel the need to own one.

There is some evidence that his wife's family might have had slaves before Lincoln knew her. Even if that was true, it would certainly not be a reflection on Lincoln.

Chapter Fourteen

Presidential Scholars

George Washington was not considered a scholar. As a little boy, he had expected to get a great education because his father was a wealthy man. But Washington's father, Augustine Washington, died when he was 48. George was only 11 at the time.

How did this impact George's education? Well, his father's money and land were divided among several heirs. George's mother could no longer afford to send George to college. There was certainly no chance for a fancy education in England, which his older brothers received.

Washington was self-conscious about his lack of schooling. He felt this even more from being around Adams, Jefferson, and Madison, all of whom were brilliant and well-educated.

Sometimes, people who are successful and poorly educated downplay the importance of school. They think that since they did not need it to succeed, it must not matter much. Washington was not that way. He wished he could improve himself academically. Back then, older people did not go to college like many do now. Even if that had been more common back then, Washington was kind of busy. He won a revolution. He served two terms as president. He ran one of the biggest business empires in the State of Virginia. That did not leave much time to go back to school.

That said, Washington really did want to sharpen his mind. He accomplished this by reading a lot. He accumulated more than 900 books in his personal library. Washington also collected pamphlets and other forms of literature. His total number of reading materials was over 1,200.

Despite Washington's lack of education, He became the chancellor of William and Mary. Do you know what a college chancellor is? I didn't, and I have worked in colleges for years.

Originally, the college chancellor was seen as someone who outranked the college president. The chancellor was usually not on the college campus. The chancellor could advise the president on big issues from afar. William and Mary University is located in Virginia. Its earliest chancellors all lived in England.

Nowadays, a chancellor is the head of one university when that university is part of a bigger system. For example, I live in Knoxville, Tennessee. The big university in my city is the University of Tennessee. It is part of an overall system that includes universities in the cities of Chattanooga, Memphis, and Martin. They are all considered the University of Tennessee. They can be referred to by their city (UT Martin, UT Memphis, etc.).

Washington served as chancellor from 1788-1799. This means he did that job while he was President of the United States! He was quite a busy man.

John Tyler was also a chancellor of William and Mary. He held this position from 1859-1862. Tyler was the chancellor after he was done being president of the country.

The only other president to serve as a college chancellor was Millard Fillmore (13th president). He led the University at Buffalo. It is unique that the school is called the University *at* Buffalo, instead of the University *of* Buffalo.

Two presidents served as the rector of the University of Virginia. They were Thomas Jefferson and James Madison.

A rector is not like a chancellor or a college president. The rector is the leading academic official. That might sound like a college presidency, but it is not. A rector is more like a vice president of academic affairs. The president is in charge of the college as a whole. This includes academics, business affairs, human resources, admissions, and student life. The rector just oversees the professors. At some schools, the professors select their rector.

Multiple United States presidents served as college presidents earlier in life. The list consists of James Garfield, Woodrow Wilson, and Dwight Eisenhower.

Garfield was the president of Hiram College. His educational path is amazing! He was a student but could not afford tuition. The school hired him as a janitor so he could pay for his classes. He was such an excellent student that by his second year, they were letting him teach. He was a student and a professor at the same time. He went from janitor to professor in one year. He finished his education elsewhere but returned to Hiram and became its president. He was only 26 when he became the leader of the school.

Woodrow Wilson was the president of Princeton University. He also served as the governor of New Jersey. Thus, he had great leadership experience before becoming President of the United States. Wilson got his Ph. D. in Political Science. Interestingly, he wrote a biography of George Washington. Do you think it is neat that a future president would write about another president? I do. They were both from Virginia. I bet that helped make Washington interesting to Wilson.

Dwight Eisenhower was the president of Columbia University. It would be hard to run a college. Eisenhower led Allied Forces in World War Two. He was in charge in North Africa first. Next, he led the war effort in Europe. I imagine running a college was easy after that.

James Buchanan was not exactly a college president. He was the president of the board of trustees at Franklin and Marshall College. A board of trustees is a group of people who help run an organization. Given how much Buchanan struggled in the White House, it might have been better for the country if he had only been the president of a board.

There is a prestigious academic award known as a Rhodes scholarship. Have you ever heard of someone who was a Rhodes scholar?

The term comes from Cecil J. Rhodes. He wrote in his will that several scholarships would be provided each year allowing people to attend Oxford University in England for two to three years. The scholarships could only go to people who were British, from former colonies that were still loosely connected with Britain, or from the United States.

Only one president was close to being a Rhodes scholar. It was Bill Clinton. But he is not considered one because he left Oxford after only one year to continue his college education in the USA. Clinton went to Yale after leaving Oxford.

George W. Bush was not excellent at giving speeches. His critics questioned his intelligence. And yet, with all the brilliant presidents we have had, Bush accomplished something that eluded the rest. Bush has degrees from two Ivy League schools. His first college degree from Yale. It was in history. He then received a Masters of Business Administration from Harvard. He is also the only president to get a MBA.

Chapter Fifteen

Vice Presidential Trivia

It is an impressive accomplishment to become a vice president. There are over three hundred million Americans alive today and only one of them is vice president. In all of American history, there have only been 49 people who have served in this office.

For most of the presidential elections in American history, two people have chosen to run together as presidential and vice presidential candidates. Originally, men were considered individually. The top vote-getter would become president. Whoever finished second would become vice president. Because of this system, we once had a president from one party and a vice president from the other. The president was John Adams, a Federalist. The vice president was Thomas Jefferson, a Democratic-Republican. As mentioned in an earlier chapter, their relationship went through a hard time during this period.

Several presidents have had multiple vice presidents. But two times in American history a vice president has served multiple presidents. George Clinton was the VP for both Jefferson and Madison. It is not surprising that he could work with both men since they had so much in common. Jefferson and Madison shared the same ideas about the government.

John C. Calhoun was another matter altogether. He served as VP for two presidents, and it did not go well.
Calhoun wanted very much to be president himself. He had served in Congress. He had also been the secretary

of war. Today, that position is known as secretary of defense.

Anyway, Calhoun tried to be president in 1824. Competition was fierce. There were four other men who also wanted the job. William Crawford is the least famous today, but he was kind of popular back then. He had served as the secretary of war and secretary of Treasury. Of all the candidates in that election, his political views were the most like Jefferson and Madison's. Henry Clay was the Speaker of the House. He had also helped negotiate the end of the War of 1812. Andrew Jackson was a war hero. John Quincy Adams worked with Clay to negotiate the end of the War of 1812. Adams had also been secretary of State. The previous three presidents had all served in that office before eventually becoming president.

Calhoun quickly decided he had no chance of becoming president that year. He instead turned his attention to the vice presidency.

Adams won in 1824, but it was controversial. No candidate had received a majority of electoral votes. Because of that, the House of Representatives had to choose the president. Adams won, even though Jackson had more votes than him.

Adams served one, unpopular term. During that term, something strange happened. Articles began to appear in a newspaper that criticized the President. That was not the strange part. All presidents get criticized.

What made it weird is it came from his own vice president! By the time of the Election of 1828, Calhoun threw his support behind Jackson. Jackson won in 1828, and Calhoun became Jackson's vice president.

Interestingly, Calhoun started having disagreements with Jackson, too. When Jackson got reelected, Martin Van Buren was his new vice president.

Calhoun was a popular and reasonably successful politician. And serving as vice president for two men is an impressive achievement. But it is interesting how Calhoun burned some bridges.

There have been several times in American history when a vice president resigned or died, and the office remained unfilled for a while. It seems strange that we have gone long periods when we have not had a vice president.

Franklin Roosevelt has been the only president to have three vice presidents. John Nance Garner was his VP for Roosevelt's first two terms. Garner was much more conservative than Roosevelt. Back in the 1930s, there were liberals and conservatives in both parties. By running together, Roosevelt and Garner helped unify the Democrats. But Garner did not really like Roosevelt's policies. Garner definitely did not like the idea of Roosevelt serving a third term. Garner decided to run for president himself in 1940. When Roosevelt won the nomination that year, he had no interest in continuing to work with Garner.

Henry Wallace served as VP for Roosevelt's third term. Sometimes when we make a change from something we do not like, we go too far in the opposite direction. Garner was seen as too conservative by some. His replacement, Wallace, was too liberal for others.

Harry Truman took over during Roosevelt's fourth term. But Roosevelt lived less than four months after his last inauguration. Truman was thrust into the presidency with little time to prepare. Also, this was during World War Two. Truman was in a tough position.

Spiro Agnew was the vice president for Richard Nixon. Agnew was forced to resign in 1973. Agnew had taken bribes while he was governor of Maryland. By the time the authorities had proof of his wrongdoing, he was already vice president. He agreed to a plea bargain. He pled "no contest" to tax evasion. He had not declared the income from his bribes on his taxes, which is why he was accused of tax evasion. To plead "no contest" means that the person is neither admitting guilt nor arguing his/her innocence.

Agnew was able to avoid going to jail, but he had to give up his job as vice president.

Geraldine Ferraro was the first female vice presidential candidate for a major party when she ran for the Democrats in 1984. She and the presidential candidate, Walter Mondale, lost badly.

Kamala Harris became the first female vice president in American history in 2020 when she was elected alongside President Joe Biden.

Chapter Sixteen

Random Presidential Trivia

Four presidents have refused to accept a salary. They were George Washington, Herbert Hoover, John Kennedy, and Donald Trump. They were already quite wealthy. Still, this was nice of them. Other rich presidents have taken a salary.

John Quincy Adams visited Europe often. He served on diplomatic teams before his presidency. He could speak seven languages! I think that is amazing.

Andrew Jackson fought multiple battles against Native Americans. Sometimes he said and did mean things to them. But he also adopted multiple Native American children. Jackson was a complicated man.

Three presidents had "Hickory" nicknames. I mentioned two of them before. Andrew Jackson was "Old Hickory". James Polk was "Young Hickory". Franklin Pierce was "Young Hickory of the Granite Hills".

Martin Van Buren (8th) wrote an autobiography. It was more than seven-hundred pages! The most surprising thing is not how long it was. Here is the big shocker: He did not mention his wife! Does that seem like a good idea to you? It does not seem like a good idea to me. She died in 1819, more than two decades before the autobiography came out.

Van Buren really did not like to talk about his deceased wife. It made him sad. One of his sons wanted to name his child after her. Because the son heard so little about her, he had to ask his dad what her name was. Van

Buren never remarried, despite living 43 years after she died.

There was a pre-Civil War president whose grandson is still alive today. (As I type this, it is the year 2022.) The president was John Tyler. Tyler had a son at the age of 63. That son was in his seventies when he fathered two children. One of those children died in 2020.

There are no presidents who were born in Tennessee. But three men moved there and lived for many years before becoming president. They were Andrew Jackson, James Polk, and Andrew Johnson (17th).

The two main political parties today are the Democratic and Republican Parties. You have already read that there was a Federalist Party. John Adams was the one and only Federalist president.

There also used to be a Whig Party. Four presidents were Whigs. Only two of the four were elected. They were William Henry Harrison and Zachary Taylor. They both died in office, and then their Whig vice presidents took over. John Tyler succeeded Harrison. When Zachary Taylor died, Millard Fillmore became the last Whig president.

Abraham Lincoln was the favorite president of Walt Disney. When Disney was a little boy, he used to dress up as Lincoln and recite the Gettysburg Address in school. Walt Disney was awesome!

I bet Chester Arthur (21st) had more pairs of pants than you do. He had 85 of them! He also had about that many pairs of shoes.

Warren Harding (29th) used to own a newspaper. He reported the news, but then he started making the news as president.

Ronald Reagan was a successful actor in movies and on TV. But there was a president before him who acted on a smaller scale. Richard Nixon used to perform in plays. He met his future wife while doing a play.

Speaking of Richard Nixon. He visited Disneyland more than any other president. He was shy and hard to get along with, but he knew a fun place to go. Disneyland is amazing.

Both Gerald Ford and Bill Clinton were adopted as little children.

Clinton made the decision to run for president one day when he was a teenager. He was inspired after he met President Kennedy. Clinton was part of a club called "Boys Nation". The club arranged for a group of its members to visit the President. Afterwards, Clinton told his friends he would be president someday. They teased him about it, but he got the last laugh.

Clinton was not the only kid who met a president and then became a president. When Franklin Roosevelt was five years old, his family visited Grover Cleveland in the White House. Many years later, Roosevelt was elected president four times.

Games!

Washington was a Dancer, Lincoln was a Wrestler

Game One

Presidents and Their Pets Quiz

1. Which president owned at least twelve dogs?
2. Some people think this president owned an alligator. Which president is it?
3. The King of Siam first offered a herd of elephants to which president?
4. There was a president whose son owned a turkey. Which president was that?
5. Rebecca the Raccoon belonged to whom?
6. Which president once starred in a movie with Bonzo?
7. Who was the president who called his dog "Bo"?

Please see the next page for the answers.

Game One

Presidents and Their Pets Quiz

Answers

1. George Washington
2. John Quincy Adams
3. James Buchanan
4. Abraham Lincoln
5. Calvin Coolidge
6. Ronald Reagan
7. Barack Obama

Game Two

Presidential Athletes Quiz

1. How many wrestling matches did Abraham Lincoln lose?
2. Which president had a future baseball player named after him?
3. Which president lived next to a golf course?
4. Which president drew up a play for an NFL team?
5. Who played center for the University of Michigan football team?
6. Who is the former president who owned a Major League Baseball team?

Please see the next page for the answers.

Game Two

Presidential Athletes Quiz

Answers

1. one
2. Grover Cleveland
3. Dwight Eisenhower
4. Richard Nixon
5. Gerald Ford
6. George W. Bush

Game Three

The George Quiz

Let's see what you remember about George Washington, George H. W. Bush, and George W. Bush. The answers are on the next page.

1. Which George was born in Virginia?
2. Which George was married to Laura?
3. Which George had stepchildren?
4. Which George was the Director of the CIA?
5. Which George did not fight in a war?
6. Which George only served one term?

Game Three

The George Quiz

Answers

1. George Washington
2. George W. Bush
3. George Washington
4. George H. W. Bush
5. George W. Bush
6. George H. W. Bush

Game Four

The James Quiz

Here is a quiz over the six presidents named "James". They are James Madison, James Monroe, James Polk, James Buchanan, James Garfield, and James Carter. James Carter was called "Jimmy". The answers are on the next page.

1.   Who was George Washington's closest friend among these Jameses?
2.   Which James never got married?
3.   Which James served in the Navy?
4.   Which two Jameses ran against each other for a seat in the House of Representatives?
5.   Which James was president during the Mexican war?
6.   Which James got shot while he was president?
7.   Which James was a peanut farmer?
8.   Which James honored his promise to only serve one term as president?

Game Four

The James Quiz

Answers

1. James Madison
2. James Buchanan
3. Jimmy Carter
4. James Madison and James Monroe
5. James Polk
6. James Garfield
7. Jimmy Carter
8. James Polk

Game Five

The John Quiz

There are four presidents who were named "John". They are John Adams, John Quincy Adams, John Tyler, and John Kennedy. Let's take a quiz about them. The answers are on the next page.

1. Which state were all of them except Tyler born in?
2. In which state was Tyler born?
3. Which one of them served as secretary of state?
4. Which one of the four never served in the United States Congress?
5. One of them was elected to the House of Representatives after being president. Who was it?
6. Which one sided with the Confederacy?
7. Which two of them switched political parties?
8. Who was the richest of these presidents?

Game Five

The John Quiz

Answers

1. Massachusetts
2. Virginia
3. John Quincy Adams
4. John Adams
5. John Quincy Adams
6. John Tyler
7. John Quincy Adams and John Tyler
8. John Kennedy

Game Six

The William Quiz

There are four presidents who were named "William," We had William "Bill" Clinton, William Henry Harrison, William McKinley, and William Howard Taft. There was also a William who ran for president three times but never won. His name is William Jennings Bryan. Let's take a quiz about them. The answers are on the next page.

1.   Which Williams were the only ones to be elected president twice?
2.   Which William was president during the Spanish-American War?
3.   One of these Williams knew Thomas Jefferson personally. Which one?
4.   The Cowardly Lion from *The Wizard of Oz* was a character that was inspired by this William. Name him.
5.   Which William ran for reelection and finished third?
6.   Which Williams were Democrats?
7.   Which William got stuck in a bathtub?
8.   There was a William who was from Arkansas. Which one was it?
9.   Which presidential Williams were the only ones to not die during their presidencies?

Game Six

The William Quiz

Answers

1. William McKinley and Bill Clinton
2. William McKinley
3. William Henry Harrison
4. William Jennings Bryan
5. William Howard Taft
6. William Jennings Bryan and Bill Clinton
7. William Howard Taft
8. Bill Clinton
9. William Howard Taft and Bill Clinton

Game Seven

Musical Presidents Quiz

1.   One of our earliest presidents used to write songs. Who was that?

2. Which president gave up playing the violin so he could devote more time to studying to be a lawyer?

3.   What instrument did Abraham Lincoln like to play?

4.   This man was president during the Spanish-American War. He also liked singing hymns. Who was he?

5.   There was a president who enjoyed playing the harmonica. Do you remember who it was?

6.   Who was the president who played the accordion?

7.   Do you remember which president played the saxophone on a TV show?

8.   Which president sang part of "Let's Stay Together" in public?

Game Seven

Musical Presidents Quiz

Answers

1. John Quincy Adams
2. John Tyler
3. violin
4. William McKinley
5. Calvin Coolidge
6. Richard Nixon
7. Bill Clinton
8. Barack Obama

Game Eight

Presidential Faith Quiz

1.   Which two presidents believed that God protected them from getting killed when they were shot at?
2.   This president never officially joined a church. However, he quoted the Bible a lot, and he attended a Presbyterian Church. Who was he?
3.   Who was the only president who used to be a minister?
4.   I mentioned two presidents who had been Sunday School teachers. Can you name them?
5.   Who were the only two presidents who were Quakers?
6.   Which man got baptized into the Presbyterian Church ten days after he was inaugurated as president.
7.   Who are the only two presidents so far who were Catholics?

Game Eight

Presidential Faith Quiz

Answers

1. George Washington and Ronald Reagan
2. Abraham Lincoln
3. James Garfield
4. Theodore Roosevelt and Jimmy Carter
5. Herbert Hoover and Richard Nixon
6. Dwight Eisenhower
7. John Kennedy and Joe Biden

Game Nine

Presidential Fighters Quiz

1.   Name the president who fought in the French and Indian War and the Revolutionary War.
2.   Which future president was wounded in the Battle of Trenton during the Revolutionary War?
3.   Name the two presidents who fought in the War of 1812 and also fought against Native Americans.
4.   Which Mexican War veteran was called "Old Rough and Ready"?
5.   Who was the future president who served in the Army during the Mexican War and the Civil War?
6.   How many future presidents fought in the Civil War?
7.   Who was the only future president to fight in the Spanish-American War?
8.   Can you name the future president who was a US Naval Cadet during World War Two?

Game Nine

Presidential Fighters Quiz

Answers

1. George Washington
2. James Monroe
3. Andrew Jackson and William Henry Harrison
4. Zachary Taylor
5. Ulysses Grant
6. There were five: Ulysses Grant, Rutherford B. Hayes, James Garfield, Benjamin Harrison, and William McKinley.
7. Theodore Roosevelt
8. Jimmy Carter

Game Ten

Presidential Friendships Quiz

1. Name at least one president who was good friends with James Madison. Can you name the other presidential friend that Madison had?
2. Who was James Monroe's favorite neighbor?
3. Which two presidential friends had nicknames with the word "Hickory" in them?
4. Who was the friend who got mad at Theodore Roosevelt for running against him for president?
5. Two presidential friends have had memes made about them together. Who were they?

Game Ten

Presidential Friendships Quiz

Answers

1. George Washington and Thomas Jefferson
2. Thomas Jefferson
3. Andrew Jackson and James Polk
4. William Howard Taft
5. Barack Obama and Joe Biden

Game Eleven

Outer Space Presidents Quiz

1.   Which president started our space program?
2.   Who was the first president to say we should go to the moon?
3.   Who was the president during all our moon landings so far?
4.   Which astronaut ran for president?
5.   Which president started the Space Force?

Game Eleven

Outer Space Presidents Quiz

Answers

1. Dwight Eisenhower
2. John Kennedy
3. Richard Nixon
4. John Glenn
5. Donald Trump

Game Twelve

Left-Handed Presidents Quiz

Can you name the six presidents who were left-handed? I will give you the first letter of the first name of each one.

J _____

H _____

G _____

G _____

B _____

B _____

Can you name the two ambidextrous presidents? I will give you the first letters of their first names too.

H _____

R _____

Game Twelve

Left-Handed Presidents Quiz

Answers

Here is a list of our left-handed presidents:

James Garfield
Herbert Hoover
Gerald Ford
George H.W. Bush
Bill Clinton
Barack Obama

Here are the names of the two ambidextrous presidents:

Harry Truman
Ronald Reagan

Game Thirteen

Presidential Myths

1. Here's the easiest question in this book: What kind of tree did young George Washington allegedly chop down?
2. Name two animals whose teeth ended up in Washington's dentures.
3. Which president was falsely accused of being an atheist?
4. Was John Quincy Adams' strangest (alleged) pet an alligator or a crocodile?
5. Which president did not like slavery but got falsely accused of owning slaves?

Game Thirteen

Presidential Myths

Answers

1. Cherry
2. You could have picked walrus, horse, and/or cow
3. Thomas Jefferson
4. Alligator
5. Abraham Lincoln

Game Fourteen

Presidential Scholars Quiz

1. George Washington served as the chancellor of William and Mary. Who was the other president to hold that office at that school?
2. At which college did Thomas Jefferson and James Madison serve as rectors?
3. Which president started as a janitor before rising through the ranks and becoming a college president?
4. Which president wrote a book about George Washington?
5. This president helped win World War Two, then he became the president of Columbia University.
6. Who was the president that earned degrees from two Ivy League schools?

Game Fourteen

Presidential Scholars Trivia

Answers

1. John Tyler
2. University of Virginia
3. James Garfield
4. Woodrow Wilson
5. Dwight Eisenhower
6. George W. Bush

Game Fifteen

Vice Presidential Trivia Quiz

1. Who was the vice president who did not belong to the same party as his president?
2. John Calhoun was the vice president for two men. Name them.
3. Which president had three vice presidents?
4. Which vice president had to resign because he broke the law?
5. The first time the Democrats ran a woman for vice president, she lost. Who was she?

Game Fifteen

Vice Presidential Trivia

Answers

1. Thomas Jefferson
2. John Quincy Adams and Andrew Jackson
3. Franklin Roosevelt
4. Spiro Agnew
5. Geraldine Ferraro

Game Sixteen

Random Presidential Trivia Quiz

1. Name any two of the men who decided they did not want to accept a salary as president.
2. Which president did not mention his wife in his autobiography?
3. There was a president who served before the Civil War whose grandson is still alive today. (As I type this, it is the year 2022.) Who was that president?
4. He fought multiple battles against Native Americans. He also adopted multiple Native American children. Who was he?
5. How many presidents used to live in Tennessee?
6. Who was the last Whig to be a president?
7. Who was Walt Disney's favorite president?
8. Which president had the most pairs of pants?
9. Which future president used to own a newspaper?
10. Which future president met his wife while acting in plays in his community?
11. Two presidents were adopted. Do you know which ones?
12. One day in the 1960s, a teenager met President John Kennedy. The teenager decided on that day that he wanted to be president. Then he went and made that happen (many years later). Who was this?

Game Sixteen

Random Presidential Trivia

Answers

1. There were four total: George Washington, Herbert Hoover, and Donald Trump.
2. Martin Van Buren
3. John Tyler
4. Andrew Jackson
5. Three—Jackson, Polk, and Andrew Johnson
6. Millard Fillmore
7. Abraham Lincoln
8. Chester Arthur
9. Warren Harding
10. Richard Nixon
11. Gerald Ford and Bill Clinton
12. Bill Clinton

Game Seventeen

Word Search

R	S	T	R	O	O	S	E	V	E	L	T	P
O	R	W	A	S	H	I	N	G	T	O	N	O
T	O	M	J	E	F	F	E	R	S	O	N	L
E	A	P	R	D	A	D	C	O	P	B	R	K
V	D	E	E	M	O	N	R	O	E	I	L	W
H	A	A	A	C	A	R	T	E	R	D	R	X
A	M	C	G	Z	O	B	H	I	G	E	S	J
R	S	H	A	M	R	U	M	O	E	N	T	A
R	T	W	N	M	R	S	T	O	P	T	R	C
I	E	I	S	E	N	H	O	W	E	R	U	K
S	M	A	D	I	S	O	N	H	I	X	M	S
O	W	H	I	T	E	H	O	U	S	E	P	O
N	C	A	R	V	S	L	I	N	C	O	L	N

White House	Washington	Roosevelt	Harrison
Jefferson	Carter	Lincoln	Jackson
Reagan	Monroe	Trump	Biden
Bush	Madison	Polk	Veto
Adams	Eisenhower		

Word Search Answer Key

```
R S T R O O S E V E L T P
O R W A S H I N G T O N O
T O M J E F F E R S O N L
E A P R D A D C O P B R K
V D E E M O N R O E I L W
H A A A C A R T E R D R X
A M C G Z O B H I G E S J
R S H A M R U M O E N T A
R T W N M R S T O P T R C
I E I S E N H O W E R U K
S M A D I S O N H I X M S
O W H I T E H O U S E P O
N C A R V S L I N C O L N
```

White House	Washington	Roosevelt	Harrison
Jefferson	Carter	Lincoln	Jackson
Reagan	Monroe	Trump	Biden
Bush	Madison	Polk	Veto
Adams	Eisenhower		

About the Author

Timothy D. Holder likes presidents, history, nice people, and Japanese food. He loves Jesus, his wife, his five step kids, and his friends. His family has two dogs, two cats, and two horses. He has written several other books. One of them is called *Presidential Trivia*.

Dr. Holder is also a public speaker. to invite him to your school, go to his website, www.tdhcommunications.com. You can also message him via Facebook.

Book Recommendations

The Citadel by M. B. Mooney is a book aimed at teens. It is an action fantasy story that revolves around a boy fighting for survival in a hostile world. I really enjoyed the story's fast pace. I also liked how the characters kept doing things that surprised me. They were not predicable, which made the book quite interesting. While I am not a teen, I thought this story was great, and I am glad there are more books in the series.

Coop Knows the Scoop by Taryn Sounders was written for ages 8-12, but I could not put it down. It is a mystery set in a small, southern town. The main characters, young Coop and his friends, are funny, interesting, and nice. I found myself wishing this was part of a series. I liked the characters and the writing that much. It has been a long time since I was 12, but I thought this book was wonderful.

Washington was a Dancer, Lincoln was a Wrestler

Washington was a Dancer, Lincoln was a Wrestler

www.ingramcontent.com/pod-product-compliance
Lightning Source LLC
Chambersburg PA
CBHW052151090426
42741CB00010B/2220